She

She

A Woman's Place in the 21st Century

SHARON DARROUX

Certainty Publishing

Copyright © 2016 by Sharon Darroux
All rights reserved. This book or any portion thereof may not be reproduced or used in any manner whatsoever without the express written permission of the publisher except for the use of brief quotations in a book review.

Printed in the United States of America

First Printing, 2016

ISBN 978-1-944185-00-8

Certainty Publishing House
www.certaintypublishing.com
USA

For my mother, Lyn Elixer Darroux

This book is made possible with the love and support of my husband and best friend, Franklin Evans, and by my friend, sister in Christ, and editor, Jeanine Goodwin.

TABLE OF CONTENTS

1. The Road Never Taken — 11
2. Eve — 19
3. A Step Down — 29
4. I Want You... Actually I Want Your... — 35
5. Hierarchy — 45
6. The Post-Modern Eve — 55
7. A Few Good Women — 63
8. Women... Default — 101
9. Women in Ministry; Women as Ministers — 109
10. Where Do We Go From Here — 119

ONE
The Road Never Taken

As girls, we learned how to be women from our mothers, from our grandmothers, and from all the women that moved in and out of our lives. As girls, we perched on top of our parents' beds and watched fascinated as our mothers put on their makeup and clothes, and fixed their hair. As girls, we eagerly anticipated the day we would be unfettered and allowed to fully embrace being the woman we always dreamed we would be, the woman our mothers dreamed we could be.

I believe my mother had these dreams for me when I was born. There is something very unique about being the first girl born into a family. The first girl sets the standard on how the girls to follow will be raised. She "breaks in" the parents' girl-raising abilities; she can be a powerful force for good or evil for her younger siblings. The responsibilities that lay on her shoulders are enormous – and typically, she will not fully recognize the weight of that responsibility until well into adulthood.

Born the first daughter and third child of my parents, I grew up on the tropical island of St. Croix. At home, my parents and siblings were loving and affectionate, so my early years were carefree and happy. There were always plenty of hugs and kisses, laughter and happiness to go around. I can even remember kissing my brothers and sister goodnight on the cheeks before going to bed just because I loved and appreciated them so much!

My family attended the largest Seventh-day Adventist Church on the island, and spent a lot of time together: at church, visiting friends and relatives, or spending Sundays at the beach.

But by the time I was nine years old, alcoholism had my father firmly in its grip, and it would never let him go. Subsequently, the environment at home took a turn for the worse. My father stopped attending church. Money for family necessities was oftentimes used to purchase alcohol, which put a terrible strain on the family, especially on my mother. And while my father's disposition remained generally loving and affectionate, our family's once idyllic life became unpredictable and full of anxiety.

Yet, through all the ups and downs, we all loved each other and my mother faithfully made sure everyone had what they needed. She never stopped treating my father with love and respect, and she encouraged my siblings and me to do the same, though we had grown bitter and restless. Year after year, she worked tirelessly to instill her five children with moral values and Bible truths.

One particular truth my mother firmly believed in was that of a woman's place in the home. It was mandatory that a woman be capable of running an efficient home. Needless to say, Mother made the job look effortless. She never seemed to be tired; she spent hours cooking, cleaning, doing laundry, and washing dishes; yet, she always had the time and energy to help us with our homework, to read to us, play with us, and then round out the evening by taking us for a peaceful nature walk in the hills that surrounded our home.

Naturally, Mother had high hopes for me, being her first born daughter and all. I was expected to embrace and excel in all the womanly tasks of the home. But I proved to be a bit of a challenge for her, mainly because I had very little interest in the domestic affairs of life. So I rebelled. I didn't rebel against being a girl; I rebelled against the idea that I was expected to perform certain tasks simply because I am a girl.

From a very young age my interests were already wide and varied… and they rarely included housework. I loved playing with my dolls, sewing and crocheting doll clothes, and playing dress up with my little sister as much as I loved climbing trees, riding bicycles, playing softball and cops and robbers with my brothers.

I can sometimes still feel Mother's frown when I would dash into the house after a time of frolicking outside "like a boy". She did not believe little girls ought to run around outside with boys playing kickball or tag. That was not ladylike at all, and Mother was the epitome of ladylikeness.

And I wanted to be ladylike.

In fact, I deeply admired the way Mother carried herself. Eventually I did learn how to be a lady, to move gracefully, to glide and not plod, to sit properly, to stand up straight, to speak properly, and to eat properly.

But household chores were a different thing entirely. I despised household chores, and my aversion to housework soon culminated into a pivotal battle between Mother and me. It happened on a summer afternoon when I was about twelve years old. Mother called me into the kitchen saying, *"Come in here and help me cook."* She then proceeded to explain to me the reason why it was important that I learn to cook. I became annoyed right away because I was right in the middle of a very intense Super Mario Brothers video game – and I was finally winning at the game!

Reluctantly handing over the video game remote controller to my brother, I approached and stood at the entrance of the kitchen, not at all pleased with this new and totally undesirable development in my life. Mother continued to calmly explain that even if I did not know or understand right now, I had to learn how to cook for my future husband.

That did it.

Up to this point I had always been a respectful child – my parents and anyone else who knew me would have readily agreed--but this time Mother had gone too far. Cook for my future husband…Has she gone mad? I thought. In the most respectful tone I could muster, I balled up my two small fists, placed them on my hips, looked defiantly at my mother, and exclaimed in no uncertain terms, *"Then I will never get married! I don't want to ever get married! So I will never have to learn to cook for any husband, EVER!!"*

I do not remember exactly what followed, though a good sound spanking would have certainly been in order. However, Mother took my outburst surprisingly well. Somehow she knew that time would tell and so she let me go. Without another word, I went back to my Nintendo while Mother finished preparing family dinner by herself.

As an adult, I have learned that my mother was right about a lot of things. Through her efforts, I was presented with opportunities that were not as readily available to her. It was because of her sacrifice that I had more freedom to choose what I wanted in life, and she always believed I could be anything I wanted to be. I wanted to be an engineer.

After high school, I left my little island home and set off for New York, and in a few years graduated with a civil engineering degree from Syracuse University. During my years in college I learned (and actually began to enjoy) cooking and baking and having a clean house. I do still have an aversion for ironing clothes… strange. But more importantly, it would be four years after graduating from college that the future husband I emphatically denounced at the tender age of twelve would come into my life.

Franklin and I were inseparable right from the start. There were never any weird, awkward moments between us, and even though we grew up in different parts of the world, in very different cultures, it was as if we had known each other our whole lives. Even now, after being married for so many years, I am still amazed that I still experience actual physical pain if we are separated for more than just a few days.

Being married, however, will put any relationship to the test, even the most well-matched ones. The adjustment of a husband and wife to each other's daily habits and customs can, at times, be difficult. Shortly after Franklin and I were married, I found it incredibly difficult to adjust to being married. It became a constant source of tension and aggravation to have someone else make life-changing decisions that affected me. I resented having to consult with Franklin before making a big decision. My fiercely independent spirit was creating disharmony in our home and was making both of us utterly miserable.

I knew that God was not happy with the discord in our home. How could Christ dwell in a home infused with so much anger and disharmony?

There was only one thing left to do.

I fell on my knees and asked God to teach me how to be a good daughter to Him, and a good wife to my husband. I promised God that I would do all that He asked of me...no matter what.

In no time at all, I was led down a road that very few women would dare venture upon, and it is certainly a road that I would never have set a toe on of my own will.

TWO

Eve

The first stop along the journey that God brought me to was the Adam and Eve saga. Ahhh, such a romantic story at first isn't it? ...Adam wakes up from deep sleep and the first thing he sees is this tall, gorgeous woman standing right in front of him – made just for him! She is radiant with the glory of God. She is exactly what Adam never knew he always wanted, Eve.

Adam and Eve were the perfect match. Eve was more than just Adam's wife; she was literally a physical part of him, his clone with a chromosomal-twist; she was his "second self". In the beginning they saw eye-to-eye on everything. What a fantasy! A married couple who were always on the same page, always in total agreement. They were one, they were equals, and they were complete.

Equal?

Yes.

I like that.

Did Adam and Eve's equality mean they were exactly the same? Is that what being equal means? I suppose most of us will quickly blurt out "Yes!", but Scripture shows otherwise. Yes, Adam and Eve were created equal, but the evidence is unmistakable: they were not exactly the same. They differed physically. He was a man. She was a woman. They had different chromosomes and different bodies designed to do very different things. Adam was taller, chiseled, and muscular; Eve was shorter, curvy, softer, and had a more delicate appearance. They also occupied different positions in life.

Different? Yes.

I will admit that I found this realization somewhat disturbing at first; but it certainly led me to the next question: Is the equality we speak of today the same as the equality established by God in Eden? I looked up the definition of equality in the dictionary,

> *"Equality is the quality or state of having the same rights, social status, etc."*

So then having equality really means being on the same level as everyone else. And who in their right mind would not want equality, to have the same rights and the same access to everything life has to offer just like everyone around them? I've never met anyone whose chief goal is to be beneath everyone else!

Equality has been all the rage for some decades now – equal rights for women, equal rights for ethnic and minority groups, equal rights for gays, for lesbians, for transgender people – we all want that equality, the opportunity to assume any role we wish in life and not to be discriminated against or prevented from attaining it. We all want it – social, economic, political, and religious equality.

Nothing wrong with that.

But what is the equality God established, especially concerning men and women? What was different about the roles of the man and of the woman before sin? What distinguished them from each other?

Some obvious differences are: Adam, the man, was created first, in the image of God and for God. Eve was created second, in the image of Adam, from Adam, and for

Adam. Adam carried within his body the genetic seed of all humanity, both male and female, and that seed has resulted in every amazing and beautiful distinction that we now see in the human race. Eve carried within her body the eggs needed to bring life to Adam's genetic seed. Each time one of her eggs combined with one of Adam's seed, a completely new and distinct human being would begin to grow inside her body!

Different positions, yet both of them invaluable to each other.

Ellen G. White showed further distinctions between the positions of Adam and Eve in their Edenic state. Eve was provided as,

"an help meet for him[Adam]"--a helper corresponding to him--one who was fitted to be his companion, and who could be one with him in love and sympathy. Eve was created from a rib taken from the side of Adam, signifying that she was not to control him as the head, nor to be trampled under his feet as an inferior, but to stand by his side as an equal, to be loved and protected by him...Adam ... was of noble height, and of beautiful symmetry. He was more than twice as tall as men now living upon the earth, and was well proportioned. His features were perfect and beautiful. His complexion was neither white, nor sallow, but ruddy, glowing with the rich tint of health. Eve was not quite as tall as Adam. Her head reached a little above his shoulders. She, too, was noble-- perfect in symmetry, and very beautiful." Adventist Home, p. 25; Spirit of Prophecy, p. 24.

We understand that the man's job was to love and protect the woman. The woman's job was to love and support the man in every way he needed. Coming from the hand of God, the union between man and woman was perfect.

So what went wrong?

How does something so perfect become so...imperfect?

The only way to make something that is already perfect imperfect is to change the perfect thing. The wonderful balance that existed between Adam and Eve, both living in perfect union, fulfilling their equal but distinct roles in perfect happiness and harmony, ends in a most unfortunate and dramatic way and basically plunged us, their offspring, into one big, confusing mess.

So exactly where did things go wrong? Most folks believe that sin began when Eve ate the forbidden fruit – and they are right. But do we ever think about the events that transpired just before the first human sinned?

The Bible says in James 1:15 that *"when lust has conceived, it brings forth sin: and sin, when it is finished, brings forth death"*. The eating of the forbidden fruit was simply the last straw. Eve had veered off of the right path a few steps back before making that most unwise decision to disobey God.

Eve's deviation from the right path began after *"the angels had cautioned [her] to beware of separating herself from her husband while occupied in their daily labor in the garden; with him she would be in less danger from temptation than if she were alone. But absorbed in her pleasing task, she unconsciously wandered from his side. On perceiving that she was alone, she felt* *an apprehension of danger, but **dismissed her fears, deciding that she had sufficient wisdom and strength to discern evil** and to withstand it. **Unmindful of the angels' caution**, she soon found herself gazing with **mingled curiosity and admiration upon the forbidden** tree. The fruit was very beautiful, and she **questioned with herself why God** had withheld it from them"* (Patriarchs and Prophets, p.53, bold and underline emphasis added by the Author).

This entire sequence is loaded!

Do you remember reading earlier that one of Adam's functions was to protect Eve? This implies, then, that Eve was designed to function best under the protection of Adam. Are we so different now? What woman would not feel safer by the side of a big burly man if his sole job was to protect her? As human beings, we function best when we have the love, support, and strength of others.

Because the bad guy, Satan, was lurking somewhere in their lovely garden estate, Eve was cautioned to stay close to Adam; otherwise she would be in danger of being deceived if caught out there alone.

But did she take the counsel of the heavenly angels? No, we are told Eve was unmindful of the angels' warning, meaning she was not aware of how important the warning was and therefore did not pay attention to it.

After she innocently and unconsciously wanders off and realizes she is no longer near her beloved Adam – she doesn't bolt back to him as she should have – instead she says to herself, "I GOT THIS."

Can you see where the path to sin started now? First her neglect of the counsel of heavenly beings, then the shaking off of any fears resulting from her forgetfulness that counsel, to finally leaning to her own understanding that she was smart enough, brave enough, and strong enough to combat Satan all by herself!

Interestingly enough, the moment Eve pats herself on the back for her smarts and prowess, where does she find herself but hanging out under the leafy branches of the Tree of Knowledge of Good and Evil, staring at its forbidden fruit and, worst of all, questioning God in her mind. Little did she know that this was all Satan needed to ensnare her. All he needs us to say is "Why, God?"

As the daughters of Eve, don't we all have to struggle with this now firmly inherited trait from time to time? We always know what is best for us (and we're usually wrong), we always think we have a good beat on things (to later find out that we didn't), we think we are so smart and can handle anything (and usually end up trying to sort out the resulting mess for years). "I Got This" is our motto.

Have you ever wondered why Eve did not eat the forbidden fruit with her husband or even after him instead of before him? Is there any significance to the timing of the events that took place? Actually, there is. In fact, the significance of Eve eating the forbidden fruit before her husband is crucial to understanding women, to understanding why we do the things we do.

Eve did not eat the fruit simply because she wanted to see what it tasted like. Think about reasons Scripture says she ate. Genesis 3:6 says, *"... when the woman saw that the tree was good for food, and that it was pleasant to the eyes, and a tree to be desired to make one wise, she took of the fruit thereof, and did eat, and gave also unto her husband with her; and he did eat."*

Eve ate the forbidden fruit first, before giving it to her husband, because she had been inspired by Satan with the same desire he had inspired in himself thousands of years before: the desire to rule as God.

Just like Satan before his fall, there was nothing wrong in Eve's life. She was happy. Her life was absolutely perfect. She had a magnificent home; she had everything she wanted and needed; and she had no concept of fear, crime, rape, murder, theft, or abuse. She had no stress, no mortgage hanging over her head, no unruly children, no meddling mother-in-law. She had an amazing and loving husband, she had direct and open communion with her Heavenly Father and Creator and His heavenly angels.

But in a few moments, in just one wrong turn, she was convinced by a talking snake to turn against her Creator and her husband. When the moment presented itself and the talking snake gave its convincing argument, Eve grasped at the chance to rule over EVERYONE – God, angels, her husband – and so she covetously ate a fruit that she had been forbidden to eat.

Oh yeah, and she did give her husband some of the fruit, afterwards; after she had attempted to secure godhood for herself. Eating the fruit first meant that Eve would have achieved "godhood" before Adam. In essence, he would no longer be the firstborn, she would be. She could rule over him because she was now a "god", specifically because she became a "god" before him.

Finally Eve was number one!

THREE

A Step Down

Or so she thought. Now, with everything all messed up (since Adam and Eve had eaten the forbidden fruit), God had to step in and make some adjustments, without which, we would all be separated from Him and lost for all eternity.

For the most part, we tend to look at the post-sin conversation between God and His creatures in Genesis 3:8-19 as harsh punishments for their sin. "Here man – take this! Here woman – take that! Here snake – no more wings for you!" But are we looking at this the right way?

The interchange between God and His creatures after sin is actually one of love, and the pronouncements made were made out of necessity. When God asked Adam how he knew he was naked, Adam immediately cast the blame of his sin on both God and his wife. All of a sudden protecting the lovely Eve was the last thing on his mind! Eve didn't have another human being to blame, so she played the "devil made me do it" card and blamed the snake!

God in infinite mercy, love, and wisdom revealed Adam and Eve how their life would change. These changes would occur because they opened the door for evil and had given a very malevolent, sadistic ex-angel (Satan) control of themselves, their children, their grandchildren, and the planet. They gave Satan the passport to the human soul, and now without God's continual supernatural intervention, every human being would be at the mercy of Satan, a merciless despot and the sole cause of suffering and misery on the earth.

One of the first changes in human life following sin is that the man would have to work hard to make a living to support his family. The days of a tranquil life where working was fun were over. A physical change in the female body after sin would cause the woman to now have great pain and suffering in child birth, and her relationship to her husband would be unbalanced – her desire would be to her husband, and her husband would rule over her. She would have to submit to his rule.

This is where we women cringe – oh how we hate that word "submit"... especially to a man! It seems so unfair; I mean, it just plain stinks!

Why should we have to pay for something Eve did way back then?

How could God do this to us?!

Why, why, why?!

Aaargh!

Okay, okay... now that we've gotten that off our chests it is time to understand the will of our Heavenly Father.

Did you know that every decision we make or avoid making, everything we bend our minds to, every activity we participate in, everything we eat, believe, or drink, makes a physiological and psychological change in our bodies? Many parents act surprised when they see their children, after a certain age, develop tastes for certain things--things that on the surface appear to come out of nowhere. Typically, these will be things that the parents themselves toyed around with, either in actuality or fantasy, many years before:

alcohol, drugs, adultery, lying, stealing, deceit, fornication, murder, theft, homosexuality, and tobacco to name a few.

It should not be so surprising, troubling as it may be, but not surprising. We imprint our genes every day and we will pass those imprints along to our children. We can choose to order our lives after Christ and turn away from our wicked ways, but those genes are still permanently imprinted. The expression or manifestation of those genes imprinted for evil can only stay dormant as we choose to live the life of Christ. This is why parents should dedicate their children to God on a regular basis. Only God's grace can override the inherited tendencies to do evil that each child naturally inherits from their parents. In fact, the more right decisions parents make, and the more they improve their positive traits, they will pass on better traits to their offspring, giving them a greater advantage in the world.

Whether decisions are good or bad, they make a genetic impression, and not just on the kids, but on the person making the decision as well. Have you ever noticed how people that participate in similar activities tend to look similar? People that are into certain crimes tend to look like the other people who also commit similar crimes. People who eat certain foods or frequent certain places tend to resemble each other. But we should strive to look like our Father in heaven.

When Adam and Eve sinned, certain physiological and psychological changes took place and became imprinted in the human genome. These imprints have compounded over the centuries as mankind has continued to add sin to sin, and these imprints will remain until Christ comes and redeems the righteous few on Earth and "shall change our vile body, that it may be fashioned like unto his glorious body" (Philippians 3:21).

The physiological changes that resulted from Eve's sin, and that plays a part in the painful birthing experiences that have been passed down to every woman, are somewhat of a mystery and the Bible appears to be silent on it. But what really grabbed my attention was the second part of God's revelation to Eve. He said her "…desire would be to her husband, and he [the husband]…would rule over [her]".

There was one word in that revelation that I could not get out of my mind, it was *desire*.

Desire
Desire Desire Desire Desire Desire Desire
Desire Desire Desire Desire Desire Desire
Desire Desire Desire Desire Desire
Desire Desire Desire Desire Desire
Desire Desire Desire Desire

Desire.

FOUR

I Want You...

Actually I Want Your...

I have to be honest, the last part of Genesis 3:16 bothered me to no end, *"… and thy desire shall be to thy husband, and he shall rule over thee."*

Being a woman and all – this passage does not exactly make me jump for joy and I think it is safe to assume my fellow sisters feel the same way. Boy, this passage is a hard pill to swallow – I mean where's the fun part?

Let's ignore the husband ruling over the wife bit for a little while, because, for the most part, the Bible is clear that men are the head of the household and God would not have set things up in this manner if it was not in the best interest of everyone on the earth – men, women, children, society, and the Church.

But the desire part? That part is kind of weird – strangely out-of-place. Let's face it, how many women walk around day after day, year after year, deeply desiring their husbands, pining for them?

I hear silence.

I have, in fact, racked my brain to come up with even a small list of women that I know who constantly desire their husbands; I have looked for women who love their man with that deep, red-hot, passionate, uncontainable, I-would do-anything-for-you-baby kind of desire the passage seems to indicate would afflict women.

I could not find one.

Not one.

I know of women who do love their husbands very much, who treat them well, and who would do anything for them.

But desire seemed ... well…it seemed out of place, it didn't fit. I had a real conundrum on my hands: Here I had in front of me the Bible saying *"thy desire shall be to thy husband"* but the evidence of that desire in the typical marital relationship was missing. I had no choice but to conclude that the generally accepted understanding of desire in this passage was incorrect.

Let's be brutally honest: Women, wives clamoring with burning desire for their man? Sorry, they are not. Just one look at the sad state of affairs between men and women is evidence enough – the lies, the cheating, the manipulation, the deception, and the ever-increasing divorce rate.

Don't be so shocked. Most women can effortlessly slip into any role that she believes a man is looking for in a woman, and yes, she can just as easily slip right out of it. We are designed to fit the man; "help meets", remember? This unique feature of the woman, when applied for good, has a very good outcome for both the man and the woman because it produces harmony. But we do live in a sinful world, and so this unique feature can be--and is often--used for selfish purposes.

Many men have been baffled as to how their women suddenly changed from being loving enthusiasts of football, basketball, wrestling, and fishing to despising the very mention of them, but this is usually because she was never into those things to begin with and only pretended to be into those things to suit her own purposes or was so caught up with the man and everything he was into that when the love dust settles she realizes that she is really not into everything he's into as before.

Not much desiring of the man here.

It was time to delve deeper into the troubling Bible text,"... *and thy desire shall be to thy husband, and he shall rule over thee.*" Genesis 3:16.

The Hebrew word translated as "desire" here in this verse is *teshuwqah*. It is used three times in the entire Bible. The first time is in the text we just read. It was spoken by God to Eve; the second reference is found in Genesis 4:7, spoken by God to Cain; and the third reference is found in Song of Solomon 7:10, spoken by the Shulamite bride to Solomon.

We will examine *teshuwqah* as spoken by God to Eve and by God to Cain.

Teshuwqah means to stretch out after, it is a longing and a desire for something. It comes from the Hebrew word, *shuwq*, which means to run after or run over, and to overflow. Here are the two passages,

God said to Eve, "*...,I will greatly multiply thy sorrow and thy conception;in sorrow thou shalt bring forth children;and thy desire shall be to thy husband,and he shall rule over thee.*" *Genesis 3:16*

God said to Cain, "*If thou doest well, shalt thou not be accepted? and if thou doest not well, sin lieth at the door. And unto thee shall be his desire, and thou shalt rule over him.*" *Genesis 4:7.*

Let's examine the two passages side by side.

Verse:	GENESIS 3:16	GENESIS 4:7
Who is speaking?	God	God
Who is being spoken to?	Eve, and subsequently all women, the daughters of Eve	Cain, and subsequently all who choose Cain's path of rebellion
What is the message?	Eve will have pain in child birth and her desire will be to her husband but he would have the rule over her	Cain will be accepted by God if he does what is right; sin's desire was to control Cain, but Cain was to rule over sin
Who has the desire?	Eve--Her desire is to her husband	Sin--Its desire is to Cain
What is this desire?	To her husband, to stretch out after him, to rule him, to overrun and overflow him	To have Cain in its grip, to rule him, to stretch out after, to overrun and overflow him
Was the desire to be realized?	No. Eve was not to give in to her desire to rule her husband.	No. Cain was not to allow sin to have rule and dominion over him.
Who was to rule?	Adam, Eve's husband.	Cain was to rule.

From this word study it seems that we have been reading Genesis 3:16 out of context – possibly for centuries! We ran off with the word "desire" and forgot to apply the Biblical principle of comparing line upon line, scripture upon scripture, allowing the Bible to interpret itself. The *teshuwqah* mentioned to Eve and Cain had nothing to do with being filled with a passionate desire for someone or something; it had to do with a deep desire to take something over, to rule and overrun something or someone.

Sin's *teshuwqah* was to rule over Cain, but he was to rule over it. Eve's *teshuwqah* was to rule over Adam, but Adam was to rule over her. The desire of women, our *teshuwqah*, is to rule over men, over our husbands, in any way we can, but we must aim to obey God and refrain from doing this. We must learn to step down and gain control of this overwhelming desire.

Now things are beginning to make sense!

Yes, just about every woman I know – married, single, divorced – has a deep, inborn and automatic desire to rule the man she loves! Eve's sin imprinted our genes, giving us the same desire that inspired her to eat the forbidden fruit, the desire to be a god over men.

The Genesis 3:16 passage is about the desire for power, the desire to rule. This unnatural desire became a natural part of women after sin, and it is deadly. God knows that in order for women to be saved this desire would have to be overcome; that we would have to succeed at humbling ourselves in this respect; that we all must overcome this sinful character trait passed onto us by our human mother

Eve; and that we each must pass the test that she failed in the Garden of Eden.

When Eve sinned thousands of years ago by attempting a unilateral coup at godhood, she put within herself and within every single female yet to be born, a permanent and deep, sin-modified genetic desire to stretch out after and rule over men. This trait is within each and every one of us Eves. It is a genetic trait passed on to every single girl since the Garden of Eden.

Because of our instinctive longing and desire to rule, to ascend and exalt our gate, women can be saved only as we humble ourselves before God and accept without editing or complaint what God has plainly stated in His Word. And it is not easy--in fact even as I write this it hurts. But remember, this is literally the first sin committed on Earth by a human being. Certainly the "Eve" rises up in me all too often and I have to fall on the grace of God to beat that desire back. But however difficult it may be, our Heavenly Father knows what is best for us, even if we cannot see or feel it right away.

Oh, I can hear the moans and groans now!

"Hey, are you trying to take us back into the dark ages?! Are you trying to undo women's rights? Would you have us uneducated, barefoot and pregnant again?"

But the real question is: were women ever supposed to have no rights, powerless to vote or to own property, uneducated and forever pregnant?

The good things in life were given by God and were always ours, but sometimes, because of sin, Satan rises in the heart of man and those things are unjustly taken away for a time. Since the introduction of sin, many have lost their lives, freedoms, rights, and property in the most inhumane and often violent ways. The injustices and inequalities in this world come from sin, not God. Where in God's word is justification for women being jobless? Uneducated? Unable to vote? Having no rights? These are things that crept into society over the centuries that should have never been there in the first place. How quick we are to blame God for all the ills of life, for all the endless discriminations that saturate the world, instead of putting the blame where it belongs: on Satan.

So then, why the seeming double standard in Genesis? Didn't God say, "There is neither Jew nor Greek, there is neither bond nor free, there is neither male nor female: for ye are all one in Christ Jesus" (Galatians 3:28)? If that is the case, why does there seem to be a hierarchy clearly laid out in the Bible?

Isn't hierarchy wrong?

FIVE
Hierarchy

Hierarchy – who needs it, right? Why can't we all just be the same? In our world, hierarchy is synonymous with injustice and inequality.

Historically people at the top of the hierarchical food chain treat the folks on the lower rungs appallingly. There is a growing number of adherents to the Robin Hood principle that it is only right to "balance" things out in the world by taking money from the rich and distributing it to the poor – eliminate hierarchy.

But is hierarchy evil? Or is it possible that what should have been a good system is used for evil in the hands of sinful beings?

There is a hierarchy in the universe. There always has been and always will be. In the hands of a just and righteous God, hierarchy is a system of perfect order, each part of creation fulfilling their distinct role to make a perfectly working system beneficial to all.

There is hierarchy in Heaven.

There is hierarchy among the angels.

There is hierarchy among the heavenly bodies, the planets, the stars, the solar systems.

There is hierarchy on earth, among mankind and among every creature.

There is hierarchy on our jobs and in our homes.

Hierarchy is everywhere; it is necessary and it is inevitable.

I remember an old news story from years back about a water-drinking contest that ended badly when one of the participants collapsed and died after drinking too much water. In trying to win a few hundred bucks, the man drank so much water that it literally overwhelmed his body, and he died. Was the water bad? Or was the water misused? Like many good things, hierarchy can be used for good or for evil.

In the beginning, there was no problem with hierarchy. Then, one particular individual starting developing a bit of a pride problem. His name was Lucifer, later to re-invent himself as the devil and Satan.

Lucifer had a big problem with hierarchy.

It started small, sin often does. It started with just a twinge of jealousy when the Godhead--Father, Son, and Holy Spirit--went into an executive-only conference to which Lucifer was not invited. He knew he had no business in this Creator-Only meeting for he was a mere creature. He knew that the Son of God was his Creator, yet Lucifer did not like not being excluded from the meeting.

And he knew he was wrong.

But knowing all this did not stop him from making the biggest mistake of his life. He took his eyes off of God and began to focus more and more on himself. After catching a few pleasing glances at his own handsome and dazzling reflection on the Sea of Glass, he grew even more dissatisfied with his position in life, noble though it was. In fact, in the hierarchy of Heaven, Lucifer held the highest position of all the created beings in the universe. But now, because of pride and envy, it was not enough, and he began to covet a position that did not belong to him, that was not for him, and that he was wholly incompetent to perform. Yet, none of this stopped him. He so desperately wanted to be God that he was willing to break the hierarchical structure of Heaven to get it – and he didn't care who got hurt in the process. And here is where it gets interesting: Lucifer did not come clean with his fellow angels and say to them,

"Hey, I know I've been telling you all this stuff about us angels being perfect and that we don't need any commandments and laws; but the truth is I want to rule all of you because, well, I kind of want to be God, and I think I'm great--better than you at least-- so please vote for me."

No, Lucifer pushed his agenda in a very sneaky way. He shrouded his true intent by leading the other angels to believe that he was trying to make a better society, a true utopia. Of course, he conveniently forgot to mention that he had no intention of being on the same level with anybody, least of all the angels, once he changed Heaven. He would force them to serve him, he wanted them to sing praises to him, to worship him, and to bow to him.

Lucifer attacked God's law because he knew that he was breaking the law by what he was doing, and he figured that if he could do away with God's law, then... well, then he could do whatever it was he wanted without consequence. But he was wrong, because *"all God's commandments are sure. They stand fast for ever and ever"* (Psalm 111:7-8).

Nevertheless, despite being counseled concerning his wrong course of action, Lucifer kept right on pushing his agenda, desperately trying to elevate himself to the same level as God. He created a big ruckus in Heaven and was finally evicted. He soon plunged our planet into a mess with the same trickery he used in Heaven, and to this day continues to wreak absolute havoc on Earth whenever and wherever he can, while nervously awaiting his impending execution.

One of the first things Lucifer did when he started down the wrong path by nursing his *teshuwqah* to rule as God was he stopped doing his job. He left his position as a covering cherub and disrupted a perfect system of harmony. All the angels in Heaven loved their lives, they loved their jobs, and they loved their positions. Everyone was completely fulfilled doing their life's work. Everyone was totally satisfied and happy. There had never been a reason ever to gripe about not having something--every single being in the universe had everything going for them exactly the way they wanted, how they wanted, and when they wanted.

But Lucifer of his own free will decided that he wanted someone else's stuff, something that did not belong to him. Not only did he fail of accomplishing his misguided mission, he fell far below the position he was created to occupy. In trying to exalt his gate, he was greatly abased. This angel, once called the morning star, a covering cherub, son of the morning, this angel who had for eons held the honor and respect of billions of righteous beings, is now a byword and an anathema in the universe.

Hierarchy

When he planted himself on the earth with the intention of destroying our first parents, Satan did not do anything brand new; he used the same tactics that he did in Heaven, which had gotten him and one third of the angels kicked out. Because Eve was not dissatisfied with her life, the devil had to deceive her into believing that she was – only that she was too ignorant to know it; and he did this by focusing on hierarchy.

Adam and Eve, though they occupied different positions, were equals before sin entered the world. Before sin, Adam was the ruler of Earth and Eve was created to help him rule. This is what is meant by help meet. Eve was made for Adam; an amazing and beautiful gift for man, she was the last of all earthly creatures to be created, and there was no being quite like her. Can you see how hierarchy had already been established right at the beginning? God made man first. The man was made for God and in the image of God. The woman was made for man in the image of man. The animals, plants, and flowers were made for the man and woman, to give them pleasure. The job of the man and woman was to take care of the animals, plants, and the earth. The man was to love, take care of, and protect the woman. The woman was to work alongside the man, helping him with his work. His mission was her mission; they did not have separate or conflicting goals.

This was Eve's position. It was not a subservient position--she was not beneath Adam, she was not his slave neither was she his servant. And while they had one and the same purposes, the woman's role in life was from the beginning created by God to be different than the man's role in life. The woman's position was not a galling yoke, and she did not grumble about being unfulfilled. She was made for this. The work she did alongside her husband completely fulfilled her and was exactly what she wanted to do and what she would have freely chosen for herself. She was thoroughly satisfied in life.

But at the Tree of the Knowledge of Good and Evil, Satan inspired in Eve a desire for a new position--a position which he led her to believe that God was holding her back from. Unfortunately, she believed the lying, talking snake rather than believing God.

After sin everything changed. One change that stands out in particular is the evil desire Satan aroused in the woman. This evil desire awakened in Eve would forever be a source of constant conflict between her and man. When she sinned and ate of the forbidden fruit, her desires, her *teshuwqah*, changed. Instead of being passionate about the position in life God had created her for, a new satanic desire had taken its place: she wanted Adam's job, and, like Lucifer, she wanted to be God, to be worshipped.

God did not change the female position to suit the sin that was committed. He simply said that women would have to, by His grace and by conformity of the will, do that which she was naturally designed to do anyway. The desire for Eve to be a god was so strong that now, the position which used to be happy and fulfilling and perfect for the woman, has become an unfulfilling, galling yoke.

So where does that leave us, the daughters of Eve, that are living in the 21st century world of feminism and equal rights for everything?

SIX
The Post-Modern Eve

Women.
We are born expecting.
We expect equal rights.
Equal pay.
Equal opportunities.
Equal treatment.

We expect to be defined by our abilities and not by our gender. We expect everyone to understand and accept that we will do what we want, when we want, where we want--no questions asked.

It would be absolutely l-u-d-i-c-r-o-u-s to ask the 21st century woman, the post-modern Eve, to stay at home and raise the children, to give up her career, her desires and dreams for anyone, especially for family.

From childhood, I viewed the world as an open door, a place where I could go anywhere and be anything I wanted to be. Nothing was closed to me. My expansive vision of life was a continued source of friction between Mother and me as they sometimes conflicted with some of the traditional female roles I was expected to assume. But I would not concede; I refused to give up the fight. My resistance was almost equal to Mother's force, and my mother is a forceful woman. The battles to mold me into the perfect woman, the perfect future wife, at times left us both bitter and exhausted.

We fought about folding clothes (*"I have to fold his clothes too!?"*); we fought about ironing clothes (*"I don't mind a few wrinkles in my skirt..."*); we fought about washing dishes (*"how come you never ask him to do it..?"*); we fought about doing laundry (*"I don't want to do laundry, I h-a-t-e doing laundry!"*); and we even fought about how I liked to play outside with "the boys", (*"why can't I go outside and play kickball today?"*).

I especially cringed when Mother quoted Psalm 144:12 to me, which seemed to be more often than not, *"...that our daughters may be as cornerstones."* She would say this to me to keep me in the house at the same moment I was running out to play, to climb trees, or to go exploring in the nearby woods. I deeply resented being "classed" and I found it unbearably crippling to limit myself in any way.

I love my mother and would not trade her for all the mothers in the world. I knew she meant well and that it was because she loved me that she was trying to teach me these needful things, and I certainly did not set out to make her job difficult. I was glad, for my mother's sake, that my sister turned out to be my mother's dream daughter. Though my sister did not limit herself, either, she was not as headstrong and militant as I was. Unlike me, she actually seemed to enjoy helping Mother in the kitchen. She was not into "boyish" things, and she was infinitely more dainty and "girlie" than I was.

Meanwhile, I continued to push the envelope, determined never to be in a position that someone else dictated, and never to come to the place where I would have to depend on anybody for survival, especially a man.

I love men; always have. I generally get along better with men than with women. I have always felt less judged and more readily accepted by men than by women. I love the way men look, think, talk, and reason. I loved and adored my father and all my brothers. When I was very young, I remember the most exciting part of the day was waiting for daddy to come home! My siblings and I would watch for my father's truck to pull into the driveway; we would then run outside to meet him with hugs and kisses. I believed my dad was the best, smartest, funniest, strongest, most handsome man in the world.

However, the safety blanket I rested in--that certainty that I would always be well cared for--was shaken when my father started drinking. And when I saw the stress and strain that my father's drinking it put on my mother, I resolved never to be in a position where I would ever have to depend on anyone for anything, ever.

In high school, I decided I would study civil engineering in college after an infuriating conversation I had with my high school algebra teacher, who seemed to have a particular disdain for all the girls in his classroom, and who, quite frankly, told me I would never make it through engineering school.

Well, he was almost right; it really was one of the toughest five years of my life! But I loved it, and I still love it! After college, I returned to St. Croix ready to start my new life as a civil engineer. My parents were proud of me and I was grateful that they loved me enough to sacrifice so much to pay for my education.

But God had other things in store for me than just a earning a college degree. Over the years, the longer I worked with men, both on construction sites and in engineering offices, the more I truly began to love and appreciate men just for being...men. In my profession, I had witnessed, from time to time, women who seemed to be in a panic as they desperately tried to compete with the men at work. These women would stomp around the office barking orders at everybody. They were so threatened by maleness that they made a sad decision at some point in their life to sacrifice their femininity in order to get ahead in the world. It was at this point that all of my mother's painstaking instructions began to spring up in my mind. I found no conflict with being feminine and doing my job well, even in a profession where women are still outnumbered by men four to one. There was no need to lose my distinctiveness as a woman to be successful. In fact, I found greater success and progress on the job because I did not sacrifice my femininity. The men I worked with enjoyed working with me and respected my femininity just as much as I enjoyed working with them and respected their masculinity.

Five years after graduating from college, I met Franklin. He exuded self-confidence, and he was very talkative, which reminded me of my father. He was super-intelligent, and had a handsomely irresistible chin dimple. In less than twenty-four hours after meeting him I fell in love with him.

We were inseparable and soon married. Three years into our marriage, things got rough. Anger and harsh words took the place of gentleness and kindness.

With things not going the way I thought they should, the Eve in me came out big time. I had always been fiercely independent, and the truth is it aggravated me to have to "consult" with Frank before I did anything. I did not want to "compromise" on decisions or "submit" to his final decision. Why did he get the final say anyway? To say we were making each other miserable would be an understatement.

Don't get me wrong, it was not all bad. But there were times when it certainly did seem like most of our time together was spent fussing and fighting about one thing or another.

We prayed earnestly to have the peace of God fill our lives as it did before. During my personal prayer and devotion, God began to show me things concerning myself. I saw that even though I may not have been wrong about certain things, I was wrong for contending with Franklin. I needed to let go. I needed to reach the point where it was okay when my husband did not do or see things exactly the same way I did, and to trust his judgment.

Though my aim was not to overtly try to rule over Frank, I did see more clearly the Eve in me. She was always there; working hard behind-the-scenes to dominate, to subtly manipulate, to cajole and edge him out here a little or over there a bit in order to get him to do what I wanted him to do. I became more conscious of why I said the things I said and why I did the things I did.

By God's grace and strength, I made a conscious decision to be humble and become my husband's supporter instead of his opponent. I refrained from constantly fighting him on every decision, and I began to respect his decisions as final, thereby respecting his position as head of our home. It became easier over time. Today our home is a peaceful, happy one, and we have been married for over twelve years now.

With this problem nipped in the bud, I wondered if had finally become a "good woman…"

SEVEN

A Few Good Women

I always thought I was good.

Most women do, I think.

In fact, men and women think that women are...well... good.

Come on... We see it on TV and read it in books and magazines, so it has to be true. Everything in life and society tells us that we women are not just good... we're better. We are the "better half", with better bodies and better brains – we are smarter, faster, funnier--you name it, we're better at it.

Then I read Ecclesiastes (KJV) 7:27-28:

"Behold, this have I found, saith the preacher,
counting one by one, to find out the account: which yet my soul seeketh, but I find not: one man among a thousand have I found;
but a woman among all those have I not found."

I had to double-check this, so I looked it up in the New International Version.

" 'Look', says the Teacher, 'this is what I have discovered: 'Adding one thing to another to discover the scheme of things – while I was still searching but not finding – I found one upright man among a thousand, but not one upright woman among them all."

Then I triple-checked (last time, I promise) in The Clear Word paraphrase:

"When I put together everything I had learned, I was hoping to find some meaning to life, but found none. I also looked for other answers but found none. I found only one man in a thousand who was truly good, but a good woman was even harder to find."

Whoa. That hurts.

So the well-known maxim "a good man is hard to find" is apparently dead on; but the second part of the maxim, according to Scripture, is virtually unknown – apparently "a good woman is even harder to find"! Society has implanted our minds, especially in America, that women are good, that women have it going on, that women are always the victim and never the cause, the reason, the problem, or the perpetrator.

This is a very dangerous position to hold. If, as women, we truly believe deep down inside that we are right and good, how can the Holy Spirit reach us? How can we be saved? From Scripture it seems that women will naturally have a harder time attaining to righteousness than men, who are barely making the cut themselves.

How can we be saved? If women continue to relate to men, who are made in the image of God, in a way that destroys his manhood, even driving him to commit sin; if women continue to divorce men at a whim, taking his children away and robbing him financially; if women continue to ruin their children by setting poor moral and physical examples as Christians, causing them to go down a path of sin, where does that leave women in the sight of a holy God?

It leaves us guilty.

Unless these sins are confessed and repented of and the wrongs made right as much as is humanly possible, then such a one will never set foot in the kingdom of God.

How many women do you know fit into this category? Women who feel completely justified in their actions towards men no matter the reason or outcome? Women who find it irrelevant that they have lied, cheated, deceived and stolen to get what they wanted?

Many years ago, I met a woman who treated her husband so harshly you'd have to be there to see it. The man was practically her slave: making her breakfast, lunch, and dinner, responding without complaint to her never-ending stream of barks and commands. Eventually, I got up the nerve to ask her about it and the response from her was, "If you knew how he treated me many years ago you would never ask me that." I was shocked. Here was a woman, who in all respects was a God-fearing person; but she was unable to forgive her husband's rough dealings with her in the past, and she was determined to punish him to the uttermost for the rest of their lives.

Because we are women, we do tend to feel that we are always right, that we are justified in any action we take, good or bad. Because we believe we are always right, we have placed ourselves beyond all help. Unless our eyes are opened to the fact that sometimes we are wrong and that being a woman is not an excuse for doing wrong, then we will never realize that it is utterly impossible for us to enter into Heaven with characters molded after the similitude of the devil.

This brings up an important point: What does it mean to be or to become a good woman? What does it take to be that rare, hard-to-find good woman in a sea of a thousand rotten ones?

Let's look at the Biblical account of Ruth.

This poor Moabite woman lived in Israel during the time of the judges and shines like a star among all women. The young, heathen descendant of Lot's incestuous progeny lived through some hard times. She married into an Israelite family who had moved to her country of Moab to escape famine. But the family did not escape death so easily. In no time at all, death struck and took away Ruth's husband, brother-in-law, and father-in-law, leaving her, her sister-in-law, and her mother-in-law penniless and without descendants.

Despite all the hardships of life, there is no record of Ruth ever complaining "poor me". While she did have family in Moab, she experienced something while living with her husband's Israelite family that made her certain that no matter what happened in life, she was not going to be left behind. Ruth made a firm decision to join herself to God's people, to become a true follower of God, and to go with her mother-in-law, Naomi, back to Israel. Deep down inside, Ruth probably also surmised that there was a very real possibility that without her help, Naomi would have a very hard time readjusting to life in Israel, alone and with no close male relatives to help her.

In those days, without a husband or sons, a woman's lot in life could be unspeakably harsh. But Ruth was unfazed. She did not shun the idea of doing any kind of manual labor if that was what it would take to care for herself and Naomi once they arrived in Israel. How many of us would go out every day into a field to scavenge scraps of grain to feed our mothers-in-law?

Not only did Ruth do this for her mother-in-law, she made a vow to Naomi before they even left Moab, and before she knew what she was getting herself into. Ruth's vow to her mother-in-law and to God mirrors the customary marriage vow of our time:

"Ruth said, 'Entreat me not to leave thee, [or] to return from following after thee: for whither thou goest, I will go; and where thou lodgest, I will lodge: thy people [shall be] my people, and thy God my God: where thou diest, will I die, and there will I be buried: the LORD do so to me, and more also, [if ought] but death part thee and me."
Ruth 1:16-17.

That gives me chills! Here was this young woman who made a vow to be there for her mother-in-law until death parted them, while today, most of us are unwilling to even keep our vows to our own spouses!

Humility was also an integral part of Ruth's character. After arriving in Israel, Naomi sent Ruth out to pick barley from the field of Boaz, a distant relative of hers. Ruth did as she was instructed, even bowing with her face to the ground when Boaz approached her. Later, in obedience to her mother-in-law, Ruth laid down at Boaz's feet while he slept in the middle of his threshing floor, and offered a marriage proposal to Boaz, which he accepted.

It was because Ruth was humble that she did not behave as though she were entitled to something, which is a struggle far too many of us have nowadays. We get upset and feel slighted if we do not get what we want when we want it. I recently read a heart-breaking story of how three teenage siblings murdered their caretaker simply because they were angry that she would not let them stay out late at night, gallivanting all over the place. What is this world coming to?

I'm sure some people back in Ruth's day had the "me-first" problem like we do today, but she didn't. In fact, after hearing about how wonderful Ruth was to her mother-in-law, total strangers praised and poured out blessings on her. It is true that some people do things so that they can be praised by others, but this was not Ruth's aim. The praises she received were the natural result that came out of her good works. She was focused on serving God and others, and due to the nature of the praise, I gather that what she did was pretty rare for back then and even rarer now. The people in the city took notice of her and were filled with admiration. It was unheard of! A childless widow's heathen daughter-in-law, who had no legal obligation whatsoever to care for her mother-in-law, took better care of the aged Naomi than most people took care of their own mothers!

Boaz married Ruth, and of course Ruth continued to be a blessing to Naomi, giving her a beautiful grandson. The townspeople, seeing how Ruth brought joy, happiness, and prosperity to Naomi after so much heartbreak and loss, later exclaimed to Naomi that Ruth was more profitable to her than if she had had seven sons!

Ruth was indeed remarkable. But she should not have been. In a town of God-fearing people, her behavior and character should have been the norm. But it wasn't. Just as the women of Ruth's day were not exempt from reaching the high standard of Christ's character, neither are the women of today. As daughters of God, we are called to be even more exemplary than Ruth. Like Ruth, we are called to fear God, honor our parents, parents-in-law, show respect to our elders, keep our vows, be humble, industrious, honorable, and kind.

Good Women Fear God

And not just good women, good people fear God--men, women, and children. But what does it mean to fear God?

Ruth married into an Israelite family that, trying to survive a famine in Israel, had settled in her native land of Moab. How long they lived in Moab we do not know. But they were there long enough for Elimelech and Naomi's two sons, Mahlon and Chilion to meet Ruth and Orpah and get married. Ruth's in-laws must have been a pretty solid family because it was through their influence that Ruth came to know, love, and fear God. We can be sure her newly found faith was tested when, one by one, the men in the family began to die, leaving her, her sister-in-law, and her mother-in-law alone and miserable.

When Naomi decided to head back to Bethlehem she told her daughters-in-law to go back to their Moabite families. After much persuasion, Orpah returned to her family. But Ruth would not budge. She was aware that if she chose to go back to her family, she would almost certainly fall back into Moab's degrading heathenism. Without a glance backwards, Ruth joined herself to God and to His people. She had found truth and was not about to let it go no matter the cost.

How different was Ruth's response to God's call than our response to God's call today! The 21st century is the century of attractions and distractions. We have more than we need and essentially everything we want in America – money, smart phones, iPads, iPods, cars, clothes, televisions, movies on demand, restaurants, vacations, concerts, malls. Even with all this people are still unhappy. Depression, suicide, murder, mass killings, theft, envy, rage, and disease run rampant. This is because the one thing we all need is the one thing we do not want, and that is the truth.

We are afraid of the truth, afraid that to accept God fully into our lives will force us to give up the things we love. We do not believe that God is actually the "rewarder of them that diligently seek Him" (Hebrews 11:6). We do not believe He will give us everything we want, even our deepest desires. We believe, deep down inside, that by following Him we will lose, that He will rip us off, that our lives will be stale, boring, drab, and fun-less.

In our innermost selves, most of us regard God, not with godly and righteous fear, but with an unholy, fearful fear. We believe that God will take something from us and not replace it with something just as good or better. But the fearful and the unbelieving folks who turn away from God because they have wrongly judged Him as one that cannot supply their every want and need, will lose everything in the end--everything in this world and in the world to come.

The more we run away from the truth, the more we focus on time-wasting distractions and attractions (social media sites, movies, TV shows, a never-ending supply of apps to download, constantly taking and posting selfies), the greater our shock will be when Christ appears in the clouds and we realize we are not ready because, instead of living in the fear of the living God and serving Him, we would have spent most of our waking moments playing with a smartphone.

The things of this world are passing away. We are told by Christ Jesus to seek the kingdom of God and His righteousness first and then all other good things we need and want will be added to our lives. What a day that will be when our Lord appears in the heavens and people will wake up and realize that the time they should have spent preparing for His coming was instead wasted on useless, selfish, and unprofitable activities. We can be sure that Ruth would have cared less about posting selfies online; it is quite clear that her main concern was to seek after the kingdom of God and His righteousness.

The chief and most honorable trait of a good woman is that she fears the Lord. If you have been a Christian for any length of time, then you have heard before that we should fear the Lord; yet rarely is it ever clearly explained exactly how one fears the Lord.

So here it is in simple terms: To fear God means to obey God and to keep His ten commandments. That's it. As you can see, it's not very complicated at all. When truth is brought to our minds, to our consciousness, or to our doorstep, and the Holy Spirit urges on us that it is right, then it becomes our duty to accept it and to do it. This means we are not supposed to expend time, intellect, and energy trying to avoid, reinterpret, or misrepresent truth in an attempt to get out of obeying it.

We honor and fear God by being law-abiding citizens of Christ's kingdom. The law of Christ's kingdom, the Heavenly Constitution, if you will, is the Ten Commandments. It is treason against God's government to move against His law in anyway. Found written in Exodus chapter 20, the law is not a potluck buffet to pick and choose from. If that was acceptable, then Christ would not have said in James 2:10, "For whosoever shall keep the whole law, and yet offend in one [point], he is guilty of all."

To fear God means to obey Him exactly the way He asks us to obey Him, to do exactly what He says to do. It is utterly despicable to God to try and pass off a cheap substitute in place of the real thing, expecting Him to be good with that.

The cheap substitute is a substitution sacrifice; something we say or do in an attempt to offer God something else in the place of what He specifically requires. Cain was the first recorded human being to offer a substitution sacrifice. As usual, God's requirement was simple: Sacrifice a young lamb. Cain chose to sacrifice fruit instead. I sometimes wonder exactly how Cain intended to sacrifice fruit? How could fruit represent the sacrifice, loss of life, the blood of our Redeemer?

Here is another person who tried to palm off a cheap substitute sacrifice. King Saul was explicitly told to wipe out the Amalekites, a hateful, heathen tribe who had passed their probationary period without repentance. Saul was also supposed to destroy every single thing that belonged to them. 1 Samuel 15:3 says, *"Now go and smite Amalek, and utterly destroy all that they have, and spare them not; but slay both man and woman, infant and suckling, ox and sheep, camel and ass."* But did Saul get rid of every Amalekitish thing? No, of course not. He decided to take it upon himself to save some of the Amalekites' 'good stuff'; and for some reason he chose to keep the Amalekite king, Agag, alive as well. When the prophet Samuel confronted Saul about his blatant and public show of disobedience, Saul quickly placed the blame on "the people". Afterwards, he lied and claimed to have saved the Amalekites 'good stuff' to sacrifice to God! Samuel's response to Saul is also for us living in these last days: to take careful heed lest we, too, fall into the same disobedience: *"And Samuel said, Hath the LORD as great delight in burnt offerings and sacrifices, as in obeying the voice of the LORD? Behold, to obey is better than sacrifice, and to hearken than the fat of rams. For rebellion is as the sin of witchcraft, and stubbornness is as iniquity and idolatry."* 1 Samuel 15:22-23.

Nothing has changed. People will continue to try and palm off cheap substitutes on God until the close of Earth's history with the coming of our Lord Jesus Christ. Many, after hearing and being convicted by the Holy Spirit of a particular truth--whether it be the Sabbath truth, or health principles, or even tithing--will often turn their backs on the truth and many times will afterward focus their time, money and energy on activities such as feeding the homeless, helping drug addicts, and engaging in some other good deed in desperate attempt to placate God with a "substitution sacrifice".

When God tells us to go across the street from our home and give our next door neighbor the book, The Great Controversy by E.G. White, and we decide to go and give them a different book or a nice piping hot loaf of fresh homemade bread, then we are no different than Cain or Saul; like them we have chosen to present God with a worthless, unacceptable "substitution sacrifice".

Whenever we choose to do something other than what God has required; whenever we toss at Him our "substitution sacrifices"--no matter how "good" the substitution, we are disobeying God and are showing by our actions that we do not fear Him.

Oh yes, the "substitution sacrifice" might truly feel all warm and fuzzy, but without asking for forgiveness, without turning away from sin and actively choosing to do God's will, warm fuzzies will not erase the fact that we are living in the presence of a holy and righteous God completely guilty of disobeying His direct order.

Those who fear God will love the truth. Leviticus 19:14 says that those who fear God will not curse the deaf nor cause the blind to stumble. This means they will not behave in a way that will cause another person to lose their soul salvation. Verse 32 of the same chapter says that those who fear God will honor the elderly. Deuteronomy 14:23

tells us that giving a tithe of our increase is to fear God. Deuteronomy 17:19 shows that we learn to fear God by reading, studying, and obeying all Scripture. And Deuteronomy 13:4 tells us that we are to walk after the Lord our God, and fear Him, keep His commandments, obey His voice, serve Him, and cleave to Him. All this is EXACTLY what Ruth did and is exactly what is required of every human being.

Good Women Honor Their Parents

Talk about being in a bind. Naomi's prospects in life were not good. Her husband was dead, her only two sons were dead, and she was a foreigner in Moab with two Moabite daughters-in-law and no grandchildren. At best, upon returning to her homeland in Israel, she may have had the good fortune to find some kind-hearted relative to help her out; but an even likelier possibility was that she would end up a beggar in the streets.

Yet, God did not forget about poor, old Naomi. Her daughter-in-law, Ruth, who accompanied her to Bethlehem, proved to be a worthy substitute for the husband and sons lost. Ruth fully dedicated herself to loving and caring for her mother-in-law for the remainder of both their lives. Because of Ruth's devoted care and faithfulness, Naomi was honored and praised by the townspeople. Never before had anyone ever seen a woman's daughter-in-law be such a blessing to them!

In today's society, we Christians tend to try and do the least amount required of us by God's law as is humanly possible. But not Ruth. She did not try to limit the fifth commandment, which says to honor our parents; instead she fully embraced and expanded this commandment to include, in every sense, her mother-in-law, Naomi, as well.

We honor our fathers and mothers by obeying and not cursing or hitting them. I have heard people say the most awful things about their fathers and mothers through the years. They seem to think that because their father or mother was mean or was not there for them in the way they needed them to be that that somehow translated into a free pass to curse their parents.

But there is no exception clause to the fifth commandment. Read Exodus 21:17 and Matthew 15:4. The word "curseth" used here in Scripture means to make light and trifling, to curse, to despise, to bring into contempt, to lightly esteem. Put simply, it means to treat a person as if they are nothing, to treat someone with disdain because you have such a low opinion of them. Regardless of what our parents did or did not do to or for us, we are commanded by God to give our fathers and mothers honor. This means it is our duty to treat our parents with reverence and respect, to guard their reputation and their name. We are to lighten their burdens in life and give them comfort as they age.

Taking our cue from Ruth, this extends beyond just our biological parents, but includes adoptive parents, foster parents, teachers, parents-in-law, grandparents, aunts, uncles, and anyone who may have acted a significant role in our upbringing.

Good Women Keep Their Vows

Oooh...now here's a topic that has a tendency to make us squirm, mostly because if there is one thing people love more than making vows, it is breaking them!

However, there is a problem with the constant vow-breaking epidemic that is running rampant in our world today. The Bible defines a good and righteous person as one who swears to their own hurt and does not go back on their word (see Psalm 15:4). In fact, we are warned in Scripture time and time again, not to make vows willy-nilly or to take vows made lightly.

However, in this day and age, people's word--their vows--mean nothing. Many rush to altars and courts to swear and vow to do this and that; most often those vows are taken lightly and made with a hidden agenda, which often includes an unspoken intent to break the vow if all else fails. Every year, men and women by the thousands stand before God and pledge themselves to each other until death parts them. But as soon as they hit rough water, they quickly break their vows and move on down the road to find someone else to whom they can make that same, now meaningless promise.

As followers of Christ, we are required, when we utter a vow, to keep our word--forever. This is not a request of God. It is a command. It is in His Word. We are never to go back on our word, neither break our vows, even if we are certain to get the short end of the stick.

To swear means to take an oath, and it comes from the Hebrew word for the number seven. So to swear literally means to "seven yourself", to make a complete oath, vow or declaration. The rate at which Seventh-Day Adventists marry-divorce-repeat is alarming! Of all the people on Earth, should we not lead in keeping our word? Once that vow is made, like it or not, we have sevened ourselves; we have made a binding oath to another human being and are obligated to keep that oath, even to our own hurt. Keeping our vows to our own hurt means, according to Scripture, we are to keep our vow even when we are being broken to pieces and being harmed by the keeping of that vow.

Whoa – vowing is no joke!

What does this say about Ruth, a young woman who, not knowing anything about the country she was moving to, not knowing if her relationship with her mother-in-law was going to stay positive or go south, made a vow to Naomi, her mother-in-law, before God? Ruth vowed to Naomi that she would live where she lived, worship the God she worshipped, die where she died, and be buried where she was buried. Ruth sevened herself and kept her vow, every word of it.

What a lesson for us today! We are so quick to make vows, especially marriage vows. These heartfelt promises are made with tears and holding of hands, and trembling voices. Yet, after making these solemn oaths, well over 60 percent of couples, Seventh-day Adventists included, break their vows.

The reasons are too numerous to mention, but the Bible lists only one reason why someone could break their marriage vow: that is if their spouse committed adultery, and even then they do not have to divorce their spouse. Aren't we suppose to forgive one another? Doesn't the person we made a binding oath to matter? Adultery is rarely the reason why people break their vows anyway; usually it is because one person gets fed up with the other and says "I'm out". And yes…everyone's spouse is the worst spouse on the planet and everyone's "marriage" more intolerable than everyone else's. I wonder if God was unaware of the intolerable situations some married couples believe they are in. Why would He give just one "out"?

God doesn't make mistakes. He thinks of everything and makes no oversight. So we can be certain that He is fully aware of the so-called "intolerable" situations, including abuse, incompatibility, and the loss of loving feelings. We can also be certain that in the eyes of God--whom we will each have to answer to in the Day of Judgment--none of these reasons justify going back on our word.

The only reason for divorce, stated more than once in Scripture, is adultery. And again, we don't have to get divorced if our spouse adulterates. Indeed, hasn't God forgiven us of much more worse crimes in our lifetime? Did God divorce our first parents after they committed spiritual adultery in the Garden of Eden? He could have, but He chose to forgive them and opened up another chance for them to be with Him. He swore a promise to give us everlasting life and salvation if we will bind ourselves to Him. God swore to His own hurt and sevened Himself to us. He came to Earth, lived a life where He was under spiritual attack 24/7 by Satan, He was ridiculed and rejected by the very people he came to save, and then died a death we deserve. He kept His word to the end. Not one of us has ever been required to keep a vow that even remotely comes close to the circumstances in which Christ did. How can we, who follow in His footsteps and who claim to be His offspring, continue to utter vows and words that have no substance?

Not only is it wrong for us to back-pedal on our word, but there is a much more serious issue on the table-- one that few are able to grasp before they end up in a mess. Not keeping our word puts us on the very dangerous ground of self-deception. By casually breaking our solemn vows, we lose the ability to perceive that it is a great sin to do so. We think we are okay, but in reality are far from right. Our ability to recognize how evil the sin of breaking our promise to someone really is tends to be especially difficult when everyone around us is also breaking their promises and socially telling us that it is okay to do this.

We have to understand what the term "word" really means. In Hebrew, word is our speech; it is described as the actual wind that comes out of our mouths; it is something said or thought. Christ is the Word. He is the Thought of God made into human flesh. He is Existence, Life, and Breath. If we are to be like Christ, if we claim to be His followers and acknowledge that one of His main attributes is that He does not change and that He keeps His Word, then we, too, are to keep our word and not change. When we mistakenly choose to do otherwise, something happens deep within us that fundamentally changes who we are.

The most common vow men and women make today is the marriage vow. It also happens to be the vow most frequently broken. We know what happens to the other person when we break our vow to them: they are usually devastated, and their life is an emotional, social and financial wreck, to say the least. But what happens to us when we break our word? Well, the first thing we should know is that we break ourselves and not just the person we gave our word to.

Our word is who we are. It is much, much more than something we blurt out while on an emotional high; our word is the person we are deep down inside. It is our substance and our being. And when we break our most solemn, heart-felt vows, the effect on us is devastating. We lied. We are not trustworthy after all. We are a person that lied under oath. We cannot be trusted to keep our word. Before the broken promise, we probably thought pretty highly of ourselves, believing that when we said something it had some degree of meaning, some truth behind it. But after breaking our vows, we have to face an ugly truth: our words mean bumpkus.

From that point on we know that everything we say and do will be....well .... subject to how we feel. From that point forward we are fully conscious that our word is unstable, meaningless, and changeable.

What a very dangerous place to be in! If we cannot keep our word to a person that we can see and touch, how can we keep our word to God? Can God trust us if we cannot keep our vows? The answer is no. A character built on the basis of "I'll keep my word IF..." will not be saved into the kingdom of God.

How much faith, love, and trust would we have in God if He kept vows the way we do?
Something to think about, isn't it?

The Christian's relationship with God deepens during trials, adversity, and hard times not because He did not already love us infinitely, but because sometimes we need to go through some things to recognize how awesome God is. Human-to-human relationships also strengthen if they maintain their bond to each other during trials, heartbreak, adversity, and hard times as well. As human beings, if we were to love and accept one other unconditionally and through every hurdle of life, our love for each other would be indescribable.

But what if God decided to renege on His promise to save us and to never leave or forsake us? What if God became fed up?

Fed up with us and our never-ending string of adulteries and fornications; the constant lying, cheating, stealing, drugs and alcohol use, abusive behavior, our disconnected way of relating to him, and our constant commandment-breaking. What if God decided He was done with us? He would maybe stay with us just a little longer, but as soon as things got bad, when poverty, disease and financial disaster strikes, He would leave, abandoning us to life in this world with no hope. What would that be like?

Yet, we do it every day, abandoning those we vowed never to leave in the arms of ruin, desperation, and hopelessness. We solemnly promise each other that we will be there in sickness and health, prosperity and poverty, in the best of times and in the worst of times, and we vow it to the death. But as soon as the bad times come, as soon as sickness and financial difficulties invade, what do we do? We break our word and abandon the one person we vowed to remain faithful to until death.

And yet we are the same people that go to bed every night counting on Christ to remain faithful to us, don't we? Indeed, Christ is truly faithful. Besides, the problem is not with Him, it is with us. Between us and Christ, we are the ones that are in danger of leaving Him, especially when we have formed characters of the promise-breaking kind.

Look at it this way: when the hard times hit, when we are prevented from buying or selling simply because we believe in keeping God's Ten Commandments; when hunger pangs gnaw at our insides and we can't see where the next meal is coming from; when we see our children starving right before our very eyes; when we lose our jobs and are thrown out of our comfortable homes into the street, and have to leave behind precious family photos and other little treasures; when our very lives are put into mortal jeopardy because of our relationship with Christ; will our characters reveal people who have been faithful to our word to the death, or will they reveal people who break their vows and abandon their post when life gets too unbearable?

Needless to say, if we choose not to love and honor our word in our earthly relationships, we will never, ever be able to keep our word to God at the most critical time in our lives--whether this time is now or in the troublous times to come.

Swearing to our hurt extends beyond the realm of the marriage vow; it encompasses all vows. When we make a vow, to God or man, it is our duty to fulfill it. If we borrowed money and swore to pay it back, (i.e., we signed on the dotted line) then we should pay it back. If we promise to give a person something, then we should give it to them. And if we have sinned and have already broken our vows, remember there is a God in Heaven that will forgive if we are truly repentant, truly forsaking sin--in this case making an end of vow-breaking. *"Whoever under the reproof of God will humble the soul with confession and repentance, as did David, may be sure that there is hope for him. Whoever will in faith accept God's promises, will find pardon. The Lord will never cast away one truly repentant soul. He has given this promise: 'Let him take hold of My strength, that he may make peace with Me; and he shall make peace with Me.' Isaiah 27:5. 'Let the wicked forsake his way, and the unrighteous man his thoughts: and let him return unto the Lord, and He will have mercy upon him; and to our God, for He will abundantly pardon.' Isaiah 55:7" (Patriarchs and Prophets, p. 726).*

A Good Woman is Humble

Being humble is the exact opposite of being prideful. Pride was Lucifer's undoing. Scripture tells us that his "heart was lifted up". Instead of being humble and thankful to God for all the freely given blessings he received on a continual basis, Lucifer instead decided to covet the position of God, a position not meant for any creature. Realizing that he was not going to get what he wanted, he became angry and belligerent--two nasty little side effects of pride. Even with the Holy Spirit working on his heart, Lucifer refused to humble himself before the Lord, and went from being one of the most loved and respected creatures in the universe to being the most hated and despised. Talk about a step down.

Imagine if Ruth had pranced into Bethlehem on her little donkey acting all high and mighty, behaving as though she were entitled to some kind of special treatment, demanding her dead husband's land and livestock immediately; how would that have gone down? Take a guess! She would have been quickly cut down to size! The Israelites in town would have been offended, and as soon as they figured out she was just some heathen, the bad treatment would have taken a turn for the worst kind of treatment. It would not have been a pretty sight.

Thankfully, this did not happen. Ruth, being led of God and having a humble spirit, did not behave in such a manner. She went about her new hometown quietly taking care of herself and Naomi as best she could. And God blessed her. The people in town loved her. God gave her a loving, righteous husband; she brought a beautiful baby boy into the world; she brought honor and happiness to poor old Naomi, and she became a direct ancestor in the human lineage of Jesus Christ.

The Bible says *"a man's pride shall bring him low: but honor shall uphold the humble in spirit"*; the Lord *"dwells in the high and holy place, with him also that is of a contrite and humble* spirit, to revive the spirit of the humble, and to revive the heart of the contrite ones"; "whosoever shall exalt himself shall be abased; and he that shall humble himself shall be exalted." Proverbs 29: 23; Isaiah 57:15; Matthew 23:12

I'm sure we have all had our prideful moments--often, those moments are soon followed by equally embarrassing and humbling moments. But when we follow in Jesus' footsteps and humble ourselves, then God Himself will exalt us. We all have to learn how to be humble. No one has to teach us anything about being prideful; that comes naturally to every human being.

As women, how do we humble ourselves? What exactly are we supposed to do? Here's what E.G. White said on the matter in Adventist Home, p. 24:

"All the work we do that is necessary to be done, be it washing dishes, setting tables, waiting upon the sick, cooking, or washing, is of moral importance. . . . The humble tasks before us are to be taken up by someone; and those who do them should feel that they are doing a necessary and honorable work, and that in their mission, humble though it may be, they are doing the work of God just as surely as was Gabriel when sent to the prophets. All are working in their order in their respective spheres. Woman in her home, doing the simple duties of life that must be done, can and should exhibit faithfulness, obedience, and love, as sincere as angels in their sphere. Conformity to the will of God makes any work honorable that must be done."

Being humble means to have a faithful, consistent behavior of modesty and meekness in everything we do and in whatever task we take up; it means to conform our will to God's will instead of being arrogant and condescending. Being humble means to have a submissive and teachable spirit when we come to God, and to be keenly aware of our unworthiness in the sight of God, and to recognize and accept His will for our lives no matter what it is. Being humble means to have respect for our husbands and the position God has placed on them, helping them achieve greatness in the work God has given them to do, instead of always working against them and thereby not doing the work God has given to us.

A Good Woman Gets Things Done

No one can argue that Ruth was not an industrious woman. She was out there in the barley fields day and night, picking grain to feed herself and her mother-in-law. It was rough on her. This was a time in history when being a woman without a close living male relative was almost akin to a death sentence. But despite the trying circumstances, Ruth was out there T-C-B: taking-care-of-business.

Being industrious is a virtue that we should all strive for. It means to work hard and is the opposite of being slothful, lazy, and always looking for a handout. Being industrious means to be constantly and habitually active and occupied in some field of useful labor. Nowadays we seem to think it cruel and unusual punishment to have to work five days a week, and we often look forward to having "paid time off" and holidays. It is interesting to note that the crime rate always increases during any major holiday. Why is that? Because people are not working. Most people have so few useful pursuits in which to occupy their time when they are not "under the clock" that when they get a few days off work, they don't know what to do with themselves. So they drink, party, smoke, eat, and then get themselves into all sorts of trouble. You know the old saying, "idle hands are the devil's workshop."

The virtue of being an industrious woman results in the type of woman that is dependable in word and action; it results in a woman that God (and man) can trust. The industrious woman can take on a project, mission, or any other task and see it through to the end. In Scripture, industrious women are highlighted as occupying many different and significant roles in society: judge, prophetess, protector of spies, queen, wife, mother, sister, daughter, aunt, cook, negotiator, farmer, nurse, realtor, business woman, midwife, seamstress, and shepherdess,.

There is a particular push in the world right now to blur the line between men and women, to show there are no differences between them. How disgusted God must be! Did He not create man and woman different right from the start, two distinct genders made to depend on each other for survival?

Here is a weird story to give you an idea of how different male and female brains are on so many levels-- neither brain is better or worse; they are just different:

After Franklin and I had been married for about four or five years, a seemingly simple incident at home taught me just how different men and women really are. In those days we lived in a tiny apartment on the third floor of an old historic building. Our apartment had an amazing view of the nearby river, but it was cramped and constantly smelled of smoke thanks to our cigarette-smoking neighbor who lived downstairs. The bathroom had an old claw foot bathtub that seemed designed to get water all over the place except inside the actual tub. Frustrated and unable to manage the water that kept soaking the floors after each shower, I came up with an ingenious method of containment: old bath towels. The idea was to place two old towels on either side of the bathtub to soak up the wayward water and keep the floors dry. The towels could then be hung up to dry after showering. The method worked beautifully--as long as it was executed properly.

On many occasions, even after discussing and showing Frank the towel-water containment system--I would come into the bathroom after he had showered and find, to my horror, that he had either not placed the towels properly to prevent water from getting on the floor or that he had spread the wrong towel on the floor--usually my clean, soft, fluffy bath towel!

Needless to say, I was more than a little unhappy about the situation and freely let him know it. This went on for at least six months to a year, and it drove me crazy! I could not understand how this man could be so precise and detailed in everything he did and yet could be so awful as to continue to use my soft, fluffy bath towel to mop water off the bathroom floor, especially when the old raggedy floor-mop towels were right there!

Then one afternoon, I happened to walk past the bathroom just as Frank was preparing to take his shower. He was standing there in the bathroom looking back and forth between my soft, fluffy bath towel and the raggedy floor-mop towel with a look of utter confusion on his face. I watched silently and almost cried as he desperately tried to figure out which towel was my bath towel and which was the floor-mop towel. He truly did not know the difference between the towels.

I learned that my husband was not trying to drive me insane on purpose or be neglectful of something that was important to me. And I was indeed amazed that he truly did not know the difference between the towels. Where I saw and felt thickness, quality, oldness of material, colors, and stitch patterns, Frank simply saw...towels.

I finally realized that he was a man and his brain literally did not, could not, retain this kind of...(for lack of a better phrase) "domestic" information; his brain was not designed for that.

I went into the bathroom, placed the correct towels on the floor for him, and told him I now understood why he mixed up the towels; I never brought up the towel mix-up again and started keeping my soft, fluffy bath towel in a different room to help reduce his confusion over the towels.

The woman of Proverbs 31 was one woman who was not fazed by multitasking. Yes, we women complain about having to do a million things at once; but the truth is we really can do a million things at once if the situation calls for it!

I seriously doubt that Naomi was biting her fingernails every day, nervously wondering whether Ruth could handle things out there, and if she was going to bring home some food or not. No, I think she fully trusted in Ruth's capabilities to handle whatever task that was set in front of her.

No matter what it is that we have to do in life, we should do it with all our might to the glory of God, and we should do it without complaint. Ruth had plenty of reasons to complain, but she never did. She made the best of her situation and trusted God; and because of her faithfulness, God greatly blessed her.

We all know that the name of the game today is to constantly complain: we are not getting paid enough, not being recognized enough, don't have enough money, don't have a good car, and on and on and on. The pervasive theme of our culture today is entitlement. We deserve the job, the big-screen TV, the newest smartphone, the biggest house; and we do not care who gets injured as we frantically try to "get it all".

Does this make God happy when the majority of Christians, especially Seventh-day Adventists, manifest this type of materialistic character? Shouldn't we be examples to the world of a people who thrive under all circumstances and who are not in the rat race of "getting things"? Was it not our Saviour that said in Matthew 6:31-33 to "...*take no thought, saying, What shall we eat? or, What shall we drink? or, Wherewithal shall we be clothed? (For after all these things do the Gentiles seek:) for your heavenly Father knoweth that ye have need of all these things. But seek ye first the kingdom of God, and his righteousness; and all these things shall be added unto you"?*

If we have to be anxious about something, it must be directed at getting righteousness, getting a character fit for Heaven, and getting others ready for Christ's return.

The time is coming when we will not be getting, but losing, and losing everything. So being attached to things can and will prove to be a fatal hindrance. In the near future, for the sake of the gospel, we will lose our jobs, the ability to provide food, clothing, and shelter for ourselves and our families, we will lose everything for the sake of Christ, so we should take time now to learn how to be content with the things we have and to have no deep attachment to things that can be taken away at a moment's notice.

How can we face the extreme circumstances just ahead, when right now we can barely contain ourselves if our smartphone falls and breaks? This is the time to fully develop and utilize all of our gifts and strengths, to strengthen our weaknesses under the guidance of the Holy Spirit.

God expects everyone, men and women, to fully use and improve the talents and gifts He has given us. He expects us to use our talents to bless others in the world, to help build up His kingdom, His spiritual house. There are so many talented people in the world today, which, instead of using their God-given talents to bless mankind, they bring a curse on mankind and on the earth.

We do not have to look too far: intelligent men and women at the helm of corporations and organizations whose main designs are to make a profit by poisoning the environment, poisoning people's bodies, poisoning people's minds, and going great lengths to suppress any and all truth that could possibly stop them.

Good Women are Honorable

What does it mean to be honorable? For a long time I wondered about this deeply enviable character which Ruth possessed. The actual word honorable comes up about thirty times in Scripture, and is first used to describe a young heathen man by the name of Shechem, who was in love with Jacob's only daughter, Dinah. You can read the story of Shechem and Dinah for yourself in Genesis chapter 34. The prophet Samuel, King David, the leprous Captain Naaman, the woman of Proverbs 31, Joseph of Arimathaea, who buried Jesus in his own tomb, and the Greek women who became Christians through Paul's ministry are all described as honorable.

An honorable person is a person who has a consistently untarnished reputation; a person of integrity, a person guided by a high sense of honor and duty. To be honorable means to live and conduct your life--publicly and privately--in such a manner that God is always honored, that others are not defrauded and caused to stumble, and to live above reproach. We probably all know at least one person in our lives that fit this bill, that person that no one can say anything bad about, and that has always been straight from the get-go.

Part of the process of being transformed into the image of Christ, is being transformed into an honorable person. And woman who is honorable is a blessing to everyone she encounters, the light of God shines through her. And though it may seem a difficult goal, being honorable is attainable to anyone who follows God's leading and decides to take Christ's character as their own.

A Good Woman is Kind

The definition of the word "kind" in Scripture is not the same as we understand "kind" to mean today. The Hebrew word for kindness is "checed", and in Scripture, kindness primarily means to have piety towards God. Secondarily it means to perform good deeds and to be merciful to our fellow man.

Kindness revolves around the attitude and manner in which we approach God, the way we conduct ourselves in His house on the Sabbath. Sometimes we get lax in our attitude towards the Creator of the universe; at times we find ourselves getting a bit sloppy in our personal relationship with Him. We are never to approach God with a light, callous attitude. E.G. White wrote in Conflict and Courage that we should always approach God with *"deep reverence and humility"* (p. 51).

Another component of kindness is how we treat each other. We are to do good deeds and to be merciful to both man and animals. It is our duty to help those who genuinely need our help, especially our parents and those who are our brothers and sisters in Christ. When we know others are in need of something and it is in our means to provide it, we should provide it and not hold back in selfishness. Ruth's mother-in-law needed her. Naomi needed help--not just someone to care for her, but she also needed companionship. This was a woman whose entire family had passed away in a few short years, maybe in a few short months. Ruth saw Naomi's need and helped her in any way she could.

We should also be careful not to confuse kindness with being "nice". They are not the same thing. Kindness is an action--doing good to others (i.e., loving your neighbor as you love yourself). The principle of love is an action brought about by the Holy Spirit working in us. And love does not always feel nice; the two are mutually exclusive. Love is doing what is in the best interest of the other person no matter what it feels like to you or to them.

Parents who, under God's guidance, discipline their child, love that child and have a desire for that child to grow up and be an honorable person in society. The parent who does not discipline their child, no matter what pathetic excuse they offer, does not love their child; and make no mistake, the child knows that their parent does not love them no matter how "nice" the parent acts. The same goes in any circumstance we might find ourselves. When a friend or family member asks for money and we know they are going to use it to buy alcohol, tobacco, or drugs, do we give the money to them because it is too uncomfortable to say 'no', or do we stand firm on principle and not help that person destroy themselves, even when that person is raging? Will we risk altering a decades-long friendship with someone who is not in the truth by giving and sharing the Three Angels' Messages with them? Or will we keep silent and selfishly enjoy our friendship knowing full-well the things coming on the earth and that our friend is wholly unequipped to face the trials ahead?

Niceness is almost always actuated by our own feelings. When not operated under the principle of love, niceness can be very selfish, self-centered, and superficial. After many years of giving Bible Studies and handing out tracts and copies of The Great Controversy, my husband and I learned that "frowners", folks whom we could see would generally not be considered a "nice" person, usually turned out to be more genuine people and less wishy-washy than "smilers". Niceness, smiling, and politeness means nothing if that nice, smiling, polite person chooses to rebel against God and His Commandments.

In the book of Genesis, Rebekah showed kindness to a complete stranger by doing a good deed for him and asking nothing in return. The man she helped turned out to be the servant of Abraham, her great uncle, and who was on a mission to find a wife for his master's son, Isaac. Rebekah not only gave the thirsty traveler water to drink, but she was thoughtful enough to give water to his thirsty camels as well. Rebekah's kindness was rewarded by God – she went on to marry a man who loved her and joined Christ Jesus' human ancestral lineage.

With so much talk of honor, and humility, and kindness, it is only natural to wonder what we default to if we choose to go the other way.

EIGHT
Women... Default

Scripture gives some amazing examples of good women, yet the Bible also sprinkles in some bad ones to show us ladies the kind of woman we should never emulate.

Some of the bad women in the Bible were evil enough to send shivers down the spine! These women utterly failed in reaching the high standard that every woman is called to attain. Women like the idolatrous, murderous Jezebel and her murderous, power-hungry daughter Athaliah; or like the money-grubbing Delilah, the deceitful Sapphira, and the blood-thirsty adulteress, Herodias.

Unfortunately for us, these women are our automatic default. That's right--every woman on the planet will, sooner or later, automatically become like these women if she does not consciously choose to fully surrender to God day by day, obey His word, and follow the examples of the good women in Scripture.

There's no way around it; the default woman is a mess! Which one of us has not operated in default mode at some point in our lives? I know I have! In default mode we are conniving, rumor-spreading, envious, prideful, power-hungry, deceptive, unstable, unloving, harsh, unkind, lazy, dishonest, selfish, foolish, a curse to men (husbands in particular), and a curse to our children; basically, an overall disgrace to our heavenly Father, especially if we walk around claiming to be a Christian.

I'll just come right out with it: The default woman is not going to make the final cut. There will be not one single default woman in Heaven, and no amount of cunning or deception will work on the Supreme Man who is Christ Jesus our Lord.

Oh yes, we like to watch the news now and again and rail on the newest disheveled woman who makes headlines for murdering her kids or for doing some other unthinkable evil; it feels good to compare ourselves with women like that because suddenly, we don't look so bad. Yeah, I might not be perfect, but at least I'm not...fill in the blank.

But there is one Judge and Lawgiver, and He cannot be fooled. "For the word of God [is] quick, and powerful, and sharper than any two-edged sword, piercing even to the dividing asunder of soul and spirit, and of the joints and marrow, and [is] a discerner of the thoughts and intents of the heart..." (Hebrews 4:12). When our time on Earth comes to an end---whether it be today or tomorrow, God will judge us not only by the things we did and did not do, but He will also judge the reasons, motives, and deep intent of why we did or did not do what He asked of us.

Scary, huh?

It should be.

I remember a conversation I had a long time ago with an acquaintance of mine; I'll call her Jane. She was very distressed over the treatment a particular dog was receiving at the hands of his owner. For at least fifteen solid minutes, Jane poured out her disgust to me about how awful the woman who owned the dog was. Frustrated, Jane did not know what she could do for the poor, mistreated little dog.

We came up with a few ideas and were soon off on a happier subject: Jane's upcoming wedding day! As we chattered on, I asked Jane--somewhat out of the blue--if she loved her fiancé. (I don't know why I asked her this.. I just did)

There was a space of silence for about five seconds. I grew uncomfortable, and felt that maybe I should have kept my big mouth shut.

Then the answer came, "Yeah, uh huh...well I like him. I know he really loves me," followed by a mischievous chuckle.

I sat on the sofa astonished as Jane flippantly described her fiancé as being amazingly loving and kind to her, a man that would do anything and everything for her. Since all of her friends were getting married; it was time for her to get married, and if she had to pretend to love this man to get what she wanted, then that's just how it was going to be.

Jane seemed to have thought of everything, because she mentioned that she could "just get a divorce if things went sour". I observed her carefully and could not detect a trace of even the remotest concern that what she was doing could quite literally destroy a man's life forever. She soon left to run some errands, still deeply distressed about a mistreated dog.

In Scripture the default woman is very often described as an adulterous woman; she cons, she flatters, and she entices men into having sex with her the moment the husband leaves town on business. She is evil and has no concern for the lives of others. The wise king Solomon describes her as hunting for precious life until the man who falls prey to her seductions is brought down to nothing, to a piece of bread. The default woman is loud and stubborn, she always has to "go out" somewhere, and she is always in everyone else's business. No matter what her awful, sinful behavior, she will defend it and will refuse to be ashamed of what she does. She is clamorous and raucous, simple and stupid; she brings her husband to open shame and causes him to age prematurely and die before his time. She tears down her own house and destroys her family by her atrocious behavior and lifestyle.

Jezebel was a default woman. She did not fear God. She refused to be ashamed of the evil things she did. In a fit of rage, she slaughtered all but one hundred of God's prophets in the land of Israel. She was certainly not an industrious woman: When she learned of some nice property that her husband wanted, but which was not for sale, she solved the "problem" by murdering the property owner and stealing his land. In the end, instead of being praised in the gates like Ruth, Jezebel was tossed out of a window by her own servants, who were probably just waiting for the opportunity, and eaten by stray dogs in the street. Some years later, her horrid daughter, Athaliah, was executed by God's servants after a futile attempt to usurp the throne of Israel.

Delilah was a default woman. She loved money and was willing to do anything to get it, including something as lowdown as selling out her man, Samson. She spent their brief relationship lying to him, deceiving him, and setting him up to be captured by the Philistines--which she eventually succeeded in doing. Because of her, Samson's eyes were destroyed and he was imprisoned by the Philistines and forced into slavery. While we do not know exactly how Delilah fared in the end, historians believe that she was present in the heathen temple of Dagon, the false Philistine fish-god, for the big celebration of Samson's capture. She probably had front row seats to the event because of the key part she played in his imprisonment. Unfortunately for her, the celebration was cut short when Samson, who had regained his monstrous strength, pushed the pillars of the heathen temple down, causing the whole building to collapse, killing everyone in it.

And there are so many other Bible examples of default women: Sapphira, who walked into church and lied about how much she was donating to the cause of God; Herodias, who pimped out her own daughter to dance for King Herod, her husband/brother-in-law, and in so doing forced his hand to murder John the Baptist, a man of God; Potiphar's wife, who became so angry that she could not seduce her husband's servant, Joseph, that accused him of rape and got him sent to prison.

Only Christ Jesus our Lord can change the natural state of a woman, a default woman, into a good and righteous woman. Only by His grace can we overcome the defaults we so easily slip into. Only Christ can sustain us and supply us with a character fit for Heaven.

So then, what happens after we let go of the default woman and become a good woman and get the urge to go out and tell others about what God has done for us – maybe becoming a preacher and pastor is the next step?

NINE

Women in Ministry, Women as Ministers

Is it the same thing?
Women in the ministry?
Women ministers?

There is an ongoing debate over this issue in the Christian church, the Seventh-Day Adventist Church included. There is a very strong push to ordain women as ministers and pastors of God's Church.

With women's rights in full swing, there does not seem to be a reason not to ordain women as pastors. Are men still trying to keep a good woman down? These days, a woman can be anything she wants to be: a doctor, an engineer, a lawyer, a teacher, a basketball player, an airline pilot...anything--except a pastor of a Seventh-day Adventist church.

And, oh, how that burns us!

How do we deal with this uber-sensitive topic? Will we go about it using our own feelings, ideas, and modern-day beliefs, or will we address the issue by the Word of God?

What will we do if our modern-day beliefs contradict the clear principles laid out in the Bible? Will we be able to let go of cherished ideas and let the Word of God reign? Or will we join the ranks of the unwise and foolishly unite our voices with those who believe the Word of God to be ancient and obsolete?

Let us never forget that above all men and women, all cultures, all nations, and all thrones there is One who sits high on the throne of Heaven, One who knows the beginning from the end, One who will bring every word, every thought, every motive, every deed, and every action into the light of examination, whether it is good or evil.

Frightening, isn't it? But history has shown us time and time again, that whenever a person or a group of people has locked onto a particular issue and has fervently pressed that issue onto society, the government, or the church, that person or group almost always turned out to have had an ulterior motive, a motive deeply rooted in their own selfish purpose. Almost always the pressed issues are dressed and pressed as something that is for the good of all. So often, it rarely turns out that way.

Now, did the women's rights movement and general modernization of culture bring about any good thing? Sure it did! It allowed many women to fully embrace and use their God-given talents to bless the world --talents that should have never been crippled in the first place by the false reasoning that women were to remain in the house barefoot, pregnant, and career-less. The Word of God never advocated such idleness of life for women. When we read Proverbs 31, we see a woman who lived centuries ago in ancient Israel, around 1066 B.C. This woman lived a life remarkably unfettered by many of the societal chains which crippled women's usefulness and talents for many centuries, particularly between the Middle Ages and the mid-twentieth century. This amazing woman was married. She had a husband who was a either a judge or other political figure, she had an unknown number of children; she took great care of her family, ran multiple successful businesses, and had impeccable organizational skills. She had a godly character and was loved and praised by everyone who knew her.

The primary claim of the women's rights movement was for it to be instrumental in throwing open the doors of opportunity to all women; in the voting world, the workplace, etc., and these were good things to open to women. But because the foundation of the movement was not founded on biblical principles, much of the good it brought about has also been almost wholly overshadowed by the terrible results in society that it created.

Unlike the woman in Proverbs 31 who sought to uplift her husband, family, and society, women who became deeply entrenched in the women's rights movement embraced a selfish, I'll do what I want, me-first attitude. Women openly denigrated the institution of marriage; birth control and abortion were promoted for the sole purpose of giving women the "freedom" to freely fornicate and adulterate without being burdened by "accidental" pregnancies. The role of men in society was looked upon with derision, and "man-hating" became popular. Many women were led to see the stability of husband-wife-child bond as a galling yoke to be cast off.

In no time at all, the divorce rate skyrocketed and has become commonplace, especially in America. Scarcely can one meet a person that has not been married at least two, three, or four times. Most of the divorces in America are pursued by women. Without pity or remorse--even with full knowledge how their own children will be destroyed-- women break up their families. And because this is now accepted as perfectly normal, even more "new normals" are searched out and accepted by society: men dressing as women, women dressing as men, men having sex with men, women having sex with women, and boys and girls are now being raised and encouraged to explore alternate genders and lifestyles and are thereby launched into lifelong confusion. Indeed, the confusion in the family and societal structures are unprecedented.

In the Seventh-day Adventist church, the divorce rate is actually higher than the average population! The remnant people of God, a people especially set apart to carry forward the last message of hope and warning to the world as contained in the three angels' messages of Revelation 14, cannot even keep their word to their own spouses.

And now the fevered push for women to become pastors. Women are angry about being "kept out of the ministry", prevented from working for God as a pastor. Many believe they are being called into the ministry.

But is it really God calling them?

Does not being a "minister" prevent a woman from ministering to someone in need?

Does not being a "minister" prevent a woman from handing a person a book or tract?

Does not being a "minister" prevent a woman from having Bible study with someone?

Does not being a "minister" prevent a woman from running a self-supporting ministry which wins souls for Christ?

Does not being a "minister" prevent a woman from working for God?

The women during the time of Christ ministered to Him and the apostles. These women worked for the saving of souls and were known as honorable and devout women, but they were not ministers, pastors, or apostles.

In fact, there is not one scripture that even alludes to there ever being a female minister, apostle, pastor, priest, or elder in the church of God.

Not one.

Were there women who held high positions the church? Oh yes! There were quite a bit of prophetesses, there were deaconesses, and one woman even served as a judge and a prophetess in Israel. There are women shown throughout Scripture as ministering to others and laboring for the souls of others.

So why not ordain women as pastors? Because the Bible clearly lays out the qualifications of a priest, pastor, bishop, elder, and deacon. The qualifications are not fuzzy or unclear, nor are they changeable, nor are they subject to the post-modern way of thinking. And, like it or not, the one glaring qualification of being a pastor, bishop, priest, elder, or deacon is: The person has to be a man.

Let's take a look.

Exodus 29:29-30 says, *"And the holy garments of Aaron shall be his sons' after him, to be anointed therein, and to be consecrated in them. [And] that son that is priest in his stead shall put them on seven days, when he cometh into the tabernacle of the congregation to minister in the holy [place]."*

Exodus 35:19 plainly states that *"the cloths of service, to do service in the holy [place], the holy garments for Aaron the priest, and the garments of his sons, to minister in the priest's office."*

1 Timothy 3:1-5 describes the office of the bishop, whom we call pastor today, *"This [is] a true saying, If a man desire the office of a bishop, he desireth a good work. A bishop then must be blameless, the husband of one wife, vigilant, sober, of good behavior, given to hospitality, apt to teach;... One that ruleth well his own house, (For if a man know not how to rule his own house, how shall he take care of the church of God?)."*

1 Timothy 3:12-13 describes the office of deacon as, *"Let the deacons be the husbands of one wife, ruling their children and their own houses well. For they that have used the office of a deacon well purchase to themselves a good degree, and great boldness in the faith which is in Christ Jesus"*

Titus 1:5-7 clears up the office of the elder which is interchangeable with the office of the bishop and pastor, *"... and ordain elders in every city, as I had appointed thee: If any be blameless, the husband of one wife, having faithful children not accused of riot or unruly. For a bishop must be blameless, as the steward of God..."*

It is obvious from these requirements that being a man is only the first step to being properly placed in such a holy office--most men do not make the count. Men who occupy, or should occupy, these offices are God's representatives. They must be blameless, have only one wife (i.e., not the multi-marrying type on his second, third, or fourth wife). His children are to be good children. The

Scriptures make it plain that if a man cannot manage his own household, then he is not qualified to lead the church of God.

It is plain to see that the requirements surrounding the offices of the bishop, pastor, elder, and deacon are not something wrapped in mystery. It is very simple to understand.

Are we smarter and more "modern" in our thinking than God? Is our Lord "behind the times"? Didn't He realize that women were going to have full rights as men in society one day and were going to demand the same from His church? Is He trying to keep us from that desirable forbidden fruit...again?

So while we women selfishly clamor to get a chair inside the holy office, have we ever stopped to think what it would really mean if women were to be ordained pastors of God's church? Is this position just another meaningless nine-to-five job that has no real backlash? Is it possible that women at the head of God's church could do irreparable harm to the cause of God and result in an innumerable loss of souls? Are Seventh-day Adventist Christian women willing to risk losing even just one soul in order to grasp at a position that was never meant for us to have?

Lucifer wanted a position that was not meant for him to have, too. Because he refused to accept God's plan for his life, he became the sole reason why billions of angels and billions of human beings will lose out on eternal life--all this loss of life simply because Lucifer said "I want that position."

Even Ellen G. White, never pastored a church and did not run around calling herself a "church elder". In gentle humility, she ministered for Christ and won many souls for the kingdom of Heaven. Even today, though long dead, she continues to win souls for Christ through her writings. She spent her entire life ministering without being a minister.

In the past few years, I've watched and listened in shock as Seventh-day Adventist men and women have stood before God's church and pervert Scripture in the most subtle ways in an effort to deceive their brothers and sisters and garner support for their unsanctified cause of women's ordination. But I should not have been in shock because Christ tells us in Jude 1:4-13, *"For there are certain men crept in unawares, who were before of old ordained to this condemnation, ungodly men, turning the grace of our God into lasciviousness,... these [filthy] dreamers defile the flesh, despise dominion and speak evil of dignities. [They] speak evil of those things which they know not: but what they know naturally, as brute beasts, in those things they corrupt themselves. [They] are spots in your feasts of charity, when they feast with you, feeding themselves without fear: clouds [they are] without water, carried about of winds; trees whose fruit withereth, without fruit, twice dead, plucked up by the roots; raging waves of the sea, foaming out their own shame; wandering stars, to whom is reserved the blackness of darkness forever."*

So where do we go from here?

TEN

Where Do We Go From Here?

There are many things in life that may not seem fair, and these things are not for us to judge. God requires of us only to love and obey Him with all of our heart, soul, mind, and strength, and to love our neighbor as ourselves. He has given us the Bible and the Spirit of Prophecy to help us make right decisions, and if we follow Him and base everything we do, say, and believe on His Word, we will never be ashamed in the last day.

Hierarchy is not an evil thing; the first being to ever make this dubious claim was Lucifer. He presented his agenda to the other angels as wanting to "make heaven better for them", but his real goal was to supplant God and force his fellow angels to worship him instead. Lucifer wanted power and was fully incapable of wielding it.

In the hands of God, hierarchy is a good and perfect thing: angels, men, women, children, animals, and plants are all are loved and cared for by God. Yet, all have different positions to fill in life.

Dissatisfaction in life comes from covetousness, from cherishing a desire to have something that is not ours to have. This dissatisfaction breeds sin. The first thing that happens when a person becomes dissatisfied with their position and begins to deeply envy another position is to stop doing their own work. The work God has for women is a great work, and it is not the work He has for men. Many will be held accountable to God for wasting the resources and time of His church that should be used towards the closing work contained in the third angels' message.

There are places and people that women can minister to simply because she is a woman. Women can get into doors that would normally be closed to men. People, both men and women, respond differently to a woman than they would to a man, and this can be a great advantage when doing God's work. None of these things are lost on God.

We are told in Scripture, that *"...godliness with contentment is great gain...". "I have learned, in whatsoever state I am...to be content...for I know both how to be abased, and I know how to abound: everywhere and in all things I am instructed both to be full and to be hungry, both to abound and to suffer need. I can do all things through Christ which strengtheneth me."* I Timothy 6:6, Philippians 4:11-13.

It took a long time to understand the ways between men and women. It will take a lifetime and a daily walk with God to overcome the inherited and cultivated tendencies that so easily veers us off of God's path.

Change begins first in the mind.

We have to truly believe God, we have to fully trust that He knows what is best for us. We have to accept what He has shown us to be true. We have to stop coveting what we think everyone is getting or not getting and focus on what God has put in our sphere of influence.

Change comes slowly.

But if we allow God to reign in our lives, it will come. Our lives will be happier, our husbands will be happier, our families will be secure.

If we are faithful, the change will come.

ABOUT THE AUTHOR

Sharon Darroux is a civil engineering project manager, freelance writer, and database designer. She grew up on the island of St. Croix, the largest of the US Virgin Islands and now lives in the Pacific Northwest with her husband, Franklin Breon Evans.

www.ingramcontent.com/pod-product-compliance
Lightning Source LLC
Chambersburg PA
CBHW030657230426
43665CB00011B/1136